Heroic Dogs

THERAPY DOGS

by Megan Cooley Peterson

Consultant: Kathy Klotz
Executive Director, Intermountain Therapy Animals/R.E.A.D.

Minneapolis, Minnesota

Photo credits: Cover and 1, ©Anna-av/iStock Photos; 2, ©Matt Benoit/Shutterstock; 3, ©Susan Schmitz/Shutterstock; 4, ©Erik Lam/Shutterstock; 5, ©Monkey Business Images/Shutterstock; 6, ©kali9/Getty Images; 7, ©Joe Amon/Getty Images; 8, ©Eric Isselee/Shutterstock; 9, ©Kevin Sullivan/ZUMAPRESS/Newscom; 10, ©ZUMA Press Inc/Alamy; 11, ©AB Forces News Collection/Alamy; 12, ©Gingo Scott/Shutterstock; 13, ©Julian Pottage/Alamy; 14, ©JG Photography /Alamy; 15, ©David Grossman/Alamy; 16, ©ZUMA Press Inc/Alamy; 17, ©Chicago Tribune/Getty Images; 18, ©Xinhua/Alamy; 19, ©REUTERS/Alamy; 20, ©Serhii Bobyk/Shutterstock; 21, ©Monkey Business Images/Shutterstock; 22, ©PJF Military Collection/Alamy; 23, ©Eric Isselee/Shutterstock

President: Jen Jenson
Director of Product Development: Spencer Brinker
Senior Editor: Allison Juda
Associate Editor: Charly Haley
Designer: Colin O'Dea

Library of Congress Cataloging-in-Publication Data

Names: Peterson, Megan Cooley, author.
Title: Therapy dogs / by Megan Cooley Peterson.
Description: Minneapolis, Minnesota : Bearport Publishing Company, [2022] | Series: Heroic dogs | Includes bibliographical references and index.
Identifiers: LCCN 2021003693 (print) | LCCN 2021003694 (ebook) | ISBN 9781636911175 (library binding) | ISBN 9781636911267 (paperback) | ISBN 9781636911359 (ebook)RM
Subjects: LCSH: Dogs--Therapeutic use--Juvenile literature. | Working dogs--Juvenile literature.
Classification: LCC RM931.D63 P48 2022 (print) | LCC RM931.D63 (ebook) | DDC 615.8/5158--dc23
LC record available at https://lccn.loc.gov/2021003693
LC ebook record available at https://lccn.loc.gov/2021003694

For more information, write to Bearport Publishing, 5357 Penn Avenue South, Minneapolis, MN 55419.

Contents

Helping Paws

A young patient lies in her hospital bed, waiting for a visitor. Her eyes light up when a furry face pokes through the doorway. The visiting dog lays its head on the girl's lap. As the girl pets her fluffy new friend, she starts to feel a little better. The visit puts a smile on her face. But what kind of dogs visit patients in hospitals? Therapy dogs are special helpers that spread joy to people.

In the late 1800s, a famous nurse named Florence Nightingale found that dogs and cats helped her patients feel better.

Therapy dogs are trained to be gentle with hospital patients.

Comforting Canines

Everyone feels sad, scared, or lonely once in a while. Therapy dogs **comfort** people who are going through tough times. Spending time with these special **canines** lets people know they're not alone. Therapy dogs can work in many different places. These helpers go to hospitals, schools, libraries, and nursing homes.

Therapy dogs in schools get kids excited about learning.

Some therapy dogs work in courtrooms. They help people feel safe while they speak to the court.

What Makes a Good Therapy Dog?

Any **breed** of dog can become a therapy dog. But not all dogs are up for the job. The best therapy dogs are outgoing and comfortable in large groups. They stay relaxed when they meet new people and greet everyone with a wagging tail. A good therapy dog needs to be gentle.

Golden retrievers and Labrador retrievers are two of the most common breeds of therapy dog.

Therapy dogs meet with people one-on-one or in big groups.

Therapy Dog Training

Before therapy dogs can begin to help people, they need to be trained. First, therapy dogs learn **obedience**. They also learn to ignore anything that might **distract** them while working, such as food or toys.

Therapy dogs in training must pass several tests. They need to show they are ready for the big job.

While a therapy dog works to comfort people, its handler works to make sure the dog is okay.

Every therapy dog is teamed up with a **handler**. The dog and handler work together to comfort people in need. A therapy dog will stay calm while it is being petted. The handler is there to give extra help when needed.

Dress for Success

When therapy dogs are on the job, they need to look the part. Some therapy dogs wear brightly colored vests that let people know they're working dogs. Others wear badges or special bandanas. But the most important things these helpers bring to work are their wagging tails and friendly faces.

Special gear helps show people that a therapy dog belongs in places where dogs wouldn't normally go.

Unlike some working dogs, a therapy dog's job is to be petted! Just be sure to ask its handler first.

Hospital Helpers

With vests on and tails wagging, therapy dogs bring joy and comfort to patients in hospitals. People who are sick or hurt may feel scared or lonely. When therapy dogs let patients pet and hug them, the people begin to feel better. The furry friends listen calmly when patients talk to them.

Scientists have found that petting dogs is good for a person's health! It causes **blood pressure** to go down, which means the heart doesn't have to work as hard.

Therapy dogs can help people of all ages.

School Buddies

These special animals also visit schools. They can help students relax while taking tests. If a student misses a lot of school, working with a therapy dog can help **motivate** them to come more often. Therapy dogs also help kids who are learning to read. Reading to a calm canine can feel less scary than reading to another person.

Therapy dogs stay quiet when kids read to them.

Therapy dogs sometimes visit schools where a student has passed away. They can help classmates feel less sad.

Therapy on the Road

Therapy dogs sometimes have to travel to do their job. Big storms and other **disasters** make people very upset. Therapy dogs go to places where those things have happened, and they work to help **survivors** feel a little bit better. You might even spot a therapy dog while *you* travel. Some therapy dogs help people feel calmer in busy airports.

Many airports have therapy dogs to make traveling feel easier.

Therapy dogs also comfort **first responders** so that they are better able to help other people.

Caring for Therapy Dogs

Therapy dogs work hard to comfort people in need. But these dogs need love and care, too. Handlers and their families make sure therapy dogs are well fed and kept healthy with exercise and regular **veterinarian** visits.

Unlike many other kinds of working dogs, therapy dogs can work for their entire lives, as long as they are healthy.

When they're at home, therapy dogs play and relax with their families.

Therapy dogs keep training for as long as they keep working. With special care, these heroic dogs can help lots of people for many years.

Meet a Real Therapy Dog

Therapy dog Gunner works with the HOPE Animal Assisted Crisis Response Dog Team. This organization helps survivors of natural disasters. Gunner was one of the first therapy dogs on the scene after a wildfire broke out in Northern California in 2018. He spent time with people who had lost their homes. Petting and hugging Gunner helped these people deal with the loss.

Gunner also comforts the friends and family of people who have gone missing.

Glossary

blood pressure a measurement of the health of the heart and blood

breed a group of dogs that look and act in a similar way

canines dogs

comfort to make someone feel safe and at peace

disasters events, such as storms, that cause terrible destruction or harm

distract to take attention away from something

first responders the first people who come to help when there is trouble

handler a person who helps to train or manage a dog

motivate to encourage someone to want to do something

obedience doing what one is told

survivors people who live through disasters or horrible events

veterinarian a doctor who cares for animals

Index

Read More

Laughlin, Kara L. *Therapy Dogs (Dogs with Jobs).* New York: AV2 by Weigl, 2019.

Murray, Julie. *Therapy Animals (Working Animals).* Minneapolis: Abdo Zoom, 2020.

Learn More Online

1. Go to **www.factsurfer.com**
2. Enter "**Therapy Dogs**" into the search box.
3. Click on the cover of this book to see a list of websites.

About the Author

Megan Cooley Peterson is an author and editor. She grew up with two lovable dogs—a German shepherd named Sheba and a golden retriever named Gus. She lives in Minnesota with her husband and daughter.